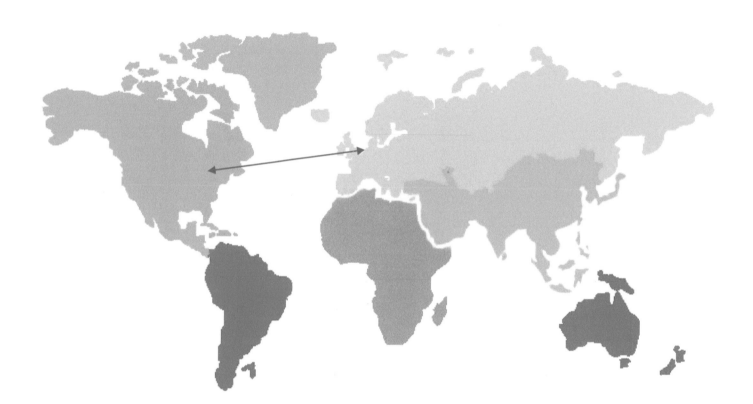

The Dutch Connection
A cookbook ? ...

Inge Zwaga

Inge Zwaga — email : backzwag@kpnmail.nl

ISBN −13 978-1729600986

All facts in this book have been checked by me. Any and all mistakes are entirely mine. Let me know if you find any and I shall correct in the next print.

Fun Fact:

If you look closely to above United States Flag you will notice that it has been created entirely with Dutch tulips !

Contents

Introduction

I s this a cookbook, a history book, a fun to read book or just a picture book? You decide, it can be whatever you want it to be !

Why *THE DUTCH CONNECTION ?* Well, because there are numerous cities with Dutch names located in the USA, some of them where the Dutch heritage is still very prominent.

Did you know for example that there are 15 Amsterdams in the USA, Tulip Festivals in Orange, Iowa and Holland, Michigan and that there are even towns where snert (traditional Dutch pea soup) is on the menu ?

For each town you will not only discover a recipe for the home cook bringing back those nostalgic flavours from times gone by, but also current American favourites with a "touch of Dutch"....

From Holland with love,

Inge

11

1

Amsterdam USA

Population : 17.758

State : New York

Website : www.amsterdamny.gov

Upon research it appeared that there is not only one Amsterdam in the USA but *15 Amsterdams !*

The smallest is Amsterdam, Indiana (Harrison County) with only 1 inhabitant in the year 2000. Dutch settlers named their town—village or community Amsterdam after their capital in the Netherlands.

The largest of the Amsterdams is Amsterdam in New York State : *small city, big heart* being their slogan. You will find the link to their website here above.

Short history : the Dutch settled in Mohawk Valley founding Schenectady in 1662 and in 1804 the name Amsterdam was

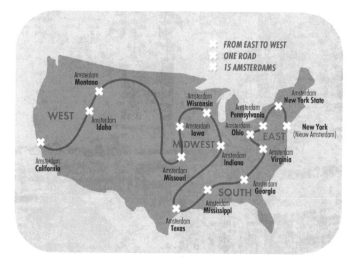

chosen in honour of these early Dutch settlers. At first the steep drop to the river hindered its development but once this barrier was overcome the city was soon transformed into a booming centre. This Amsterdam became the 7th largest city in the state of New York.

Several famous people were born in Amsterdam such as Kirk Douglas the actor and Raymond Tomlinson who is known as the inventor of the e-mail.

Apart from the many events held in this city, the culture and the local history, tourists are also able to experience its multi-culturalism including amongst others, native American Mohawk Indians and the unique Amish community. In order to receive a good impression of this appealing city (with a Dutch windmill emblem on their corporate seal.....) why don't you take a listen to "**here come the good old days**" a song written and performed by Mike Zumbola

https://youtu.be/NoJF3DV8iJM

The Montgomery County Chamber of Commerce is the official tourism promotion agency for Montgomery County in upstate New York and each year a Chili cook-off Contest is organised by the Van Alstyne Homestead Society and Museum. See also : www.facebook.com/VanAlstyneHomestead

Hence my own Chili con carne recipe on the next page.

Fun Amsterdam USA Fact:

Two Dutch filmakers , Rogier van Eck and Rob Rombout made a road movie tracing these 15 Amsterdams in the USA, which is called "Amsterdam Stories USA" see the website https://amsterdamstoriesusa.wordpress.com/

Chili con carne

Serves 4 p. or more

Preparation 10 minutes

Cooking time 20 minutes

Shopping list

1 can of chili beans (14 oz. or 400 g)
2 tablespoons of olive oil
1 lb (500 g) ground beef
7 oz. or 200 g diced salami
2 onions chopped
3 garlic cloves finely chopped
1 can of diced tomatoes (14 oz. or 400 g)
3 teaspoons mild chili powder
5 sundried tomatoes in oil
2 tablespoons tomato puree
Optional : some fresh tomatoes if in stock

My own fast chili recipe :

Preparation

Heat the olive oil and fry the ground beef together with the diced salami, the chopped onions and 1 chopped garlic glove until brown.

Once all the beef has browned add the can of diced tomatoes (and the fresh tomatoes if preferred), the tomato puree and the 2 other chopped garlic gloves and stir until you have a thick sauce.

Then mix with the chili beans and add the chili powder and chopped sundried tomatoes.

Let it simmer for about 15 minutes. Add pepper and salt to taste. Serve with a salad and slice of bread.

Enjoy !

Your personal notes

....

....

....

....

Amsterdam NL

Population : 1.350.000

Province : Noord Holland

Website : www.amsterdam.nl

Even though the Dutch government is located in The Hague; it is the city of Amsterdam that is the capital of the Netherlands. Whilst in Amsterdam you can visit the renowned coffee shops (which is where legal soft drugs can be found for sale) and of course take a look at the famous Red Light District, neither of which is much to be proud of in my opinion. However on the other hand a visit to the newly restored Rijksmuseum and the Anne Frank huis for example is to be highly recommended. During your visit to Amsterdam discover other hidden gems within the city : hire an electric boat (whisper boat) and admire Amsterdam from the water : the so called canal ring has been on the Unesco World Heritage List since 2010.

Amsterdam's nickname is "Mokum" which comes from the Jewish language, Hebrew and can be heard in Dutch children's songs such as "Brand in Mokum" which is the Dutch version of the children's song London's Burning.

Begijnhof 30, Amsterdam

Should you become fed up with the hectic city life : pay a visit to Begijnhof 30, where the tourists are requested to remain silent during their stay. This old garden, created somewhere in the mid 14th century is surrounded by the most beautiful facades. Inhabitants at this address were known as Begijntjes, a Catholic sisterhood who lived like nuns, although not having taken any vows and devoted their lives to charity. Today the houses are still habited by single women.

Amsterdam is a city of contrasts : you are still able to find places of tranquillity amongst the hustle and bustle of the centre and at the other extreme the most exciting destinations to visit and explore !

Kroket en bitterballen

Croquette and "bitterballs"

(deep fried crunchy ragout balls)

For approx. 10 croquettes and a few "bitterballs"

Preparation 3 hours for the cooked meat,
15 minutes for the ragout,
4 hours waiting time,
15 minutes to form the croquettes and/or "bitterballs",
2 hours resting time

Frying time 4 minutes

Shopping list
1 lb (500 g) stewing steak
1 shin of beef
1 pot ready to use meat stock
1/2 cup of butter (100 g)
3/4 cup of all purpose flour (100 g)
2 eggs
1 1/4 cup bread crumbs (150 g)
1 tablespoon milk
Worcester sauce
Nutmeg
Fresh or frozen parsley
Pepper and sea salt

Preparation

Place the stewing steak, the meat stock and the shin of beef into a pan with a sturdy base, add a little water (half a cup) and bring to the boil. Let this simmer for about 3 hours. You will be left with approx. 0,7 litres of stock. Separate the meat from the broth and dice the meat into very small pieces.

Melt the butter in the pan, then add the flour a little at a time and let it cook about 3 minutes until the roux has a sandy texture and becomes a thick paste. Slowly add the cold broth and stir gently until you have a smooth ragout. Further add the meat and parsley and let it simmer slowly for 4 minutes. Add pepper, sea salt, nutmeg and a few drops of Worcester sauce to taste.

Place the ragout in a flat dish or shallow container and let it cool down for at least 4 hours in the fridge.

Place the bread crumbs into one deep plate and beat the 2 eggs with a little milk into another deep plate. If you have an ice cream scoop then make a small ball of the ragout and roll it lightly through the bread crumbs after which you can further roll it into a "bitterball" or a croquette shape. Roll the balls or croquettes through the beaten eggs and finally once again through the breadcrumbs. The balls and croquettes must be completely covered on all sides.

Place them in the fridge again for about 2 hours.

Now it is time to heat the oil in your deep-fat fryer up to 350F/180C. Fry until golden approx. 4 minutes, just a few at a time (3 or 4).

Very tasty with a little French mustard.

Tip : if you have made too many you can easily deep freeze the unfried croquettes and "bitterballs" for another time.

Fun Dutch (food) fact:

A "bitterbal" received its name as originally it was served together with a glass of herb gin, which was called a "bittertje". It was and still is a nice little snack during happy hour.

Brielle USA

A Community by the River

Population : 4.774

State : New Jersey

Website : www.briellenj.com

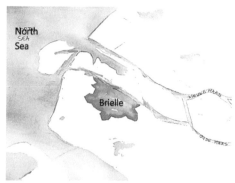

Brielle, New Jersey was originally part of Shrewsbury Township and the first settlers being Dutch and English were mostly farmers. In the 19th century the area started to develop as a summer destination.

In 1881, a group of investors formed the Brielle Land Association and purchased 150 acres of farmland between Debbie's Creek and Mud Pond. This land was divided into individual purchase lots for use as vacation homes. One of the investors suggested Brielle as a name for this area, after Brielle in the Netherlands. He thought that there was a resemblance to the Dutch town - which he had visited - due to both being close to the sea (see the drawings) and an abundance of windmills at both locations.

Today there is another similarity : every year Brielle NL celebrates the capture of the city by the Sea Beggars (see page 16) and in Brielle USA each year on the first Saturday after Labor Day in September "Brielle Day" is also celebrated. Since the first Brielle Day in 1973 it is said : "it never rains on Brielle Day !"The event has continued to grow from just a few thousand spectators in the early 70's to over 20,000 visitors nowadays. There is amongst others music, contests, ancient crafts, a vintage car show and fire engine rides for kids. The children sell sarsaparilla (a soft drink originally made from the Smilax regelii plant and considered in the 19th century as a remedy for skin and blood problems) and as such are fund raisers for the Union Landing Historical Society. If you ever have the chance : visit Brielle Day !

Photo's courtesy Mr. John Belding

Brielle is pleasantly situated on the Manasquan river . There is one church (formerly the Dutch reformed church) and there is an18 hole golf course. Many inhabitants have careers in New York as it is only 60 miles away by railroad !

Tuna mousse

Tonijnmousse

Serves 4 p. or more

Preparation 10 minutes

Shopping list

1 can of tuna in oil (5 oz. / 145 g)

1 package of plain cream cheese
(7 oz. / 200 g)

2 teaspoons capers

2 to 3 sundried tomatoes finely
chopped

1 cucumber

2 to 3 cherry tomatoes

Sambal = red pepper sauce

small appetizer glass

Preparation

Drain the oil from the can of tuna and place in a bowl. Finely mash the tuna. Add the cream cheese. Stir until nice and smooth. Add capers and sundried tomatoes.

To garnish

Dice 2 inches of cucumber, peeled and seeds removed.

Finely dice the cherry tomatoes. Add a little "sambal" and salt and pepper to taste.

Mix gently and put the bowl in the fridge for a short time which will enhance the development of flavours.

Presentation

Serve in a small appetizer glass; add the cucumber tomato mix on the bottom of the glass and top it with the tuna mousse.

Use any leftovers on a bread roll decorated with a rocket salad.

Enjoy !

Your personal notes

....

....

....

....

Fun Dutch (Food) Fact:

Alcohol:
Gin was invented in the Netherlands. It was - and still is - called "jenever" (pronounced yeh-nay-ver) and was originally used for medicinal purposes in the 16th century. The juniper berry, which is used to mask the flavour, comes from the juniper bush, a protected plant.

Brielle NL

Population : 16.350
Province : Zuid Holland
Website : www.brielle.nl

1 April

The population of Brielle re-enact their ancient history !

Each year on the 1st of April the capture of the city by the Sea Beggars is remembered. This date refers to the beginning of the rebellion against Fillips II (80 year war).

The people of Brielle re-enact the notable events of 1572. As the Sea Beggars anchor alongside Den Briel, you will meet monks, street musicians and inhabitants of the town.

The liberation from the Spanish oppressors is celebrated by means of street theatre performances, canon shots and the enactment of the demolition of the city gates by the Sea Beggars. The Spanish army is lethally decimated by marauding Beggars, chopping soldiers into pieces and leading to the absolute climax of the hanging of the Spanish commander...

Go and visit, an event not to be missed!!

Brielsche zandtaartjes

Sand Cakes from Brielle

The taste of Brielle

For approx. 15 sand cakes

Preparation 10 minutes

Dough resting time 15 minutes

Baking time 25 minutes

Shopping list

1 1/4 cup all purpose flour (150 g)

1/4 teaspoon salt

1/3 cup brown sugar (75 g)

1 packet of vanilla sugar (0.32 oz./9 g)

1 stick margarine or butter (1/2 cup or 115 g)

Preparation

Stir the flour into a bowl together with the sugar, the vanilla sugar and 1/4 tsp. salt. Cut the butter into small pieces with 2 knives and add to the other ingredients.

Knead the ingredients until you have a flexible, elastic dough. Let it rest for 15 minutes in a cool place. Meanwhile preheat the hot air oven to 338F/170 C.

Divide the dough into cookie moulds making sure the dough is pressed firmly to the edges creating a small cup.

Place the moulds on the baking tray in the middle of the oven for approx. 20 –25 minutes until golden.

Enjoy !

Your personal notes

....

....

....

....

Harlingen USA

Population : 65.665

State : Texas

Website : www.myharlingen.us

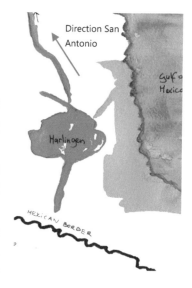

Direction San Antonio

Gulf of Mexico

Harlingen

MEXICAN BORDER

Nestled close to the Mexican border you will find Harlingen, Texas, USA. Why is this town called Harlingen, I wondered?

There is also another Harlingen in New Jersey but this is just a semi-rural community with a couple of stores and a few houses.

Harlingen, Texas having a population in excess of 65.000 has become the second largest city in Cameron County. It is also said to be the town with the lowest cost of living in the U.S. !

But how did it get it's name ?

Norman Rozeff, a local Harlingen historian wrote an article about it in the Valley Morning Star. Harlingen was named by Lon C. Hill—it's founder — as a probable honour to his friend Uriah Lott's (the railroad builder in the region) ancestral home in Harlingen, New Jersey or perhaps in honour of Lott's grandmother Elizabeth Van Harlingen.

Nowadays the nicest place to visit would be the downtown district as it is known for a number of murals on the buildings as well as an elaborate ceramic mural.

Also the area is renowned for its many antique stores.

The regional specialties are mostly Mexican food, therefore you will find my Dutch version of a Mexican meal on the next page. Hope you like it !

Photo's : courtesy of Mr. Norman Rozeff

Chicken enchiladas plus ...

Kip tortilla's plus ...

Serves 4 p.

Preparation 20 minutes

Cooking time 15 minutes

Shopping list

For the filling
14 oz. (400 g) boneless chicken
9 to 10 oz. (250 g) button mushrooms
2 cloves garlic
1 can chili beans (14 oz. or 400 g)
8 medium flour tortillas
Iceberg lettuce
1 bag of cream and onion tortilla chips
Grated cheese

For the salsa
4 tomatoes
1 or 2 shallots
Ketchup
Hot chili sauce

For the guacamole
1 ripe avocado
1 tablespoon crème fraiche
1 tablespoon mayonnaise
1 clove garlic
Cajun spices

Preparation

Dice the chicken into 1/2 inch pieces and slice the button mushrooms. Heat 2 tablespoons of oil in a medium sized frying pan and fry the chicken on high heat until golden brown. Add mushrooms and 1 clove garlic and fry for a further couple of minutes. Lower to a medium heat and add the chili beans with sauce and add pepper and salt to taste.

Salsa

Slice the tomatoes into small pieces, finely chop the shallots, mix them together with the ketchup and chili sauce and add some pepper and salt to taste.

Guacamole

Peel the avocado and remove the stone. Mash the avocado, crème fraiche, mayonnaise, the crushed garlic clove and the Cajun spices until smooth.

Place some iceberg lettuce leaves on the tortilla (preheated for 30 seconds in a microwave), some hot chicken/bean filling, a little crème fraiche and some grated cheese and roll it. Serve salsa, guacamole and tortilla chips on the side and : bon appetite !

Harlingen NL

Population : 15.769

Province : Friesland

Website : www.harlingen-friesland.nl

Harlingen

Harlingen, located in the province of Friesland and approx. 116 km from its capital Leeuwarden, is the 9th city of the renowned *Eleven City Tour*. Each winter many enthusiastic Dutch skating fans are hoping for the coldest of winters. One so cold that the brooks, rivers and canals freeze over with ice forming to a minimum depth of 6" (15 cm). Only when the ice is this thick it is safe enough for the approx. 124 miles (199 km) of the *Eleven City Tour* to finally take place at which point 300 elite skaters and 15.000 amateurs take to the natural ice. The last tour took place back in 1997 and was won by Henk Angenent, a well known Dutch marathon skater. The very first tour was mentioned as far back as 1760 but the first official race was won by Minne Hoekstra in 1909.

Since 1912 there has also been a 149 miles (240 km) *Eleven Cities Cycle Race* which has taken place almost every year. Due to its popularity it ceased to be an official race and became a general tour. This tour starts and ends in the Frisian town of Bolsward. My grandfather was lucky enough to complete the tour in 1913 ((see his "diploma" and below a picture of his arrival times in each city).

Skates manufactured by L.K. Hoekstra in Warga belonging to my mum Mieke Hoekstra

In 1986 using the pseudonym W. A. van Buren, our sports loving King Willem Alexander (then heir to the throne) on completing the race fell into his mother's arms (then Queen Beatrix) to the cheering of an enthusiastic crowd !

Detail of the Cycle Diploma

Snert or Erwtensoep

Green pea soup

This soup is traditionally eaten in wintertime when it is cold and is really a meal in itself.

Preparation

Place the spareribs, bacon, mixed vegetables, diced celeriac and the dried split green peas into the pressure cooker. Add water until all ingredients are just covered. Cook for 50 minutes.

Remove the pressure and transfer the soup into a standard soup pan. Add the smoked sausage and stock cubes to taste and let it gently warm through.

When you serve the soup remove the spareribs and bacon, putting them aside on a plate. Set the table with a soup dish for everyone, together with a small plate for the Frisian rye bread. Divide the meat from the spareribs and bacon and serve on the rye bread. The soup with the sausage slices is served in the soup dishes.

D E L I C I O U S !

P.S. the soup is often considered to being even tastier the following day ....

Serves 4– 8 p.

Preparation 10 minutes

Cooking time 50 minutes (in the pressure cooker)

Shopping list

1,5 cup dried split green peas (250 g)

1,5 lb spareribs (750 g)

1/2 lb bacon, one thick slice (250 g)

1 sack of sliced mixed vegetables for pea soup or for vegetable soup

1 medium celeriac diced or
1/2 large celeriac diced

1 smoked sausage or 4 thick Frankfurters

Stock cubes

Rye bread from Friesland

Your personal notes

....

....

....

....

Fun Dutch Fact:

Dutch people are the tallest in the world with an average height of 184 cm (6 feet) for men and 171 cm (5,6 feet) for women. This must be because of the good food of course ....

Holland USA

Population : 36.000

Province : Michigan

Website : www.cityofholland.com

Thanks to the Holland Area Convention & Visitors Bureau (www.holland.org) and their Executive Director Mrs. Sally Laukitis, I have learned how the amazing influence of our Dutch ancestors is still present in Holland Michigan ! One outstanding monument is the grain-grinding windmill De Zwaan which was brought over all the way from Vinkel, the Netherlands (near Den Bosch) in 1964. This windmill -transported in 700 numbered pieces- now proudly stands in the Windmill Island Gardens, Holland. It was reconstructed piece by piece and nowadays you can purchase the flour at the windmill shop. The mill is surrounded by beautiful gardens which boast a vista of over 100.000 tulips each spring. It was honoured by Prince Bernhard of the Netherlands, who presided over the opening ceremonies in 1965.

In Holland you can eat Dutch pastries, such as "saucijzenbroodjes" at the famous DeBoer Bakkerij & Dutch Brothers Restaurant owned by 5th generation Dutch immigrant bakers.

Typical Dutch artefacts and products such as wooden clogs and Delft's Blue ceramics are manufactured in Holland and the Nelis' Dutch Village family park is a replica of a village in the Netherlands from about 100 years ago.

Photo's courtesy Holland Area Convention & Visitors Bureau

Each year from the first Saturday in May The Tulip Time Festival celebrates Holland's Dutch heritage with 8 days of events and special attractions including 3 parades, 800 costumed "klompendancers" (clog dancers) and millions of tulips !

And did you know that the Dutch Royal family has visited Holland on several occasions ? Queen Juliana came as early as 1952 !

This lovely city is located approximately 11 kilometres from Lake Michigan where at the edge of the 145 km wide lake you will find white sandy beaches and towering sand dunes. This is an idyllic location where you can spend leisure time swimming, fishing, kayaking and boating on the lake. It is said that from this point you can see some of the most spectacular sunsets all year round.

There are several beautiful parks in the area such as Holland State Park and Tunnel Park where you must walk through a concrete tunnel in order to get to the beach. Then of course there is the "Big Red" the most photographed lighthouse in Michigan demonstrating classic Dutch architecture. In downtown Holland you will find cobblestone sidewalks, Victorian streetlights and over 90 local shops, galleries and restaurants. During winter these downtown streets and sidewalks remain snow and ice-free, thanks to the largest municipally run "snowmelt" system in the United States !

Spice nuts

Kruidnoten

Serves 10 p.

Preparation 20 minutes

Baking time 15 minutes

Shopping list

1/2 cup butter (150 g)

1/2 cup brown sugar (125 g)

1 tablespoon "speculaas" spices (10 g)

1 cup of self-rising flour (250 g)

Salt

4 tablespoons milk

In winter Sinterklaas also arrives in Holland on his white horse, just as he does in the Netherlands, he might even be a competitor or colleague of Santa Claus as they both offer presents !

When Sinterklaas offers his presents however (5th of December) they are often accompanied with spice nuts or pepper nuts. Therefore you will find the spice nuts recipe here below.

Preparation

Preheat the oven to 320F/160C. Mix the butter with the sugar, the "speculaas"spices and the flour with a 1/4 teaspoon salt. Add 4 table spoons of milk to the dough until smooth. Place parchment paper on the baking plate.

Make long rolls of the dough. Cut them in equal small parts to form little balls, the size of a marble and place them on the baking plate. Bake them for approx. 15 minutes until browned. Remove them from the oven and let them cool down completely.

Enjoy !

There is a difference between pepper nuts and spice nuts : The pepper nuts are chewy, have the appearance of small blocks and look similar to the Dutch "taai taai". Honey and aniseed are added to the rye flour. Really nice too, but different.

Holland NL

Population : almost 7 million

Province : Noord and Zuid Holland

Website : www.noord-holland.nl

www.zuid-holland.nl

Keukenhof

The Netherlands is often referred to as Holland, although in fact this is not quite right : Holland is made up of two provinces of the Netherlands : North and South Holland. Through the ages these two provinces have been considered the most powerful territories in the Netherlands with Amsterdam in North Holland being the country's capital and The Hague in South Holland where the government is seated and where the royal family resides.

Kinderdijk

You can find everything that is commemorated in the city of Holland USA in both provinces : Dutch cheese is to be found at the cheese market in Alkmaar, tulips everywhere during the spring months but look out especially for the Keukenhof Park near Lisse, the windmills at Kinderdijk, traditional costumes in Volendam and Marken and the famous Dutch gables found on the older houses. If you want to see the Netherlands in miniature : pay a visit to Madurodam in South Holland where you are able to view all of the Netherlands' important and characteristic buildings, landmarks and heritage in miniature form. Important events are highlighted such as Dutch liberation day of World War II and the third Tuesday in September (Prince's Day) when the King visits The Hague in his golden carriage and addresses Parliament with the sovereign speech from the throne.

Madurodam
3rd Tuesday in September

Madurodam
Liberation by the Allied

Hachee

Beef stew with onions

Serves 4 p.

Preparation 15 minutes

Cooking time : 2,5 hours or more

Shopping list

1,5 lbs cubed beef (750 g)

1 tablespoon olive oil

2 tablespoons butter

4 sweet onions sliced in rings

salt and pepper

1 tablespoon of all purpose flour

2,5 cup of boiling water (600 ml)

1 beef bouillon cube

4 tablespoons of apple cider vinegar

2 teaspoons of granulated sugar

2 bay leaves

3 cloves, crushed

Preparation

Preheat the oven at 300F/150C. Heat the oil and the butter in a large pan. Season the meat with salt and pepper. Fry the beef cubes on a high heat (if necessary in two batches depending of the size of your pan). Once well browned remove them from the pan and keep them warm. Add more butter to the pan and fry the onions with a pinch of salt on medium temperature until soft and golden. Add the meat, sprinkle with the flour. Fry for a further minute or 2 and stir well.

Add the hot water, beef bouillon cube and vinegar until almost submerged. Add the bay leaves, sugar and cloves. Cover the pan and place in the oven for approx. 2,5 hours.

Season to taste.

Serve with cooked potatoes and vegetables of choice. Red cabbage is a favourite however I serve this dish with stewed pears. Delicious !

Your personal notes

....

....

....

....

Fun Dutch Fact:

It is said that 75% of the world's flower bulb production comes from the Netherlands

Leyden USA

Population : 711

State : Massachusetts

Website : www.http://townofleyden.com

While searching for Leyden, USA you may come across several places with this name such as the unincorporated community of Leyden, Colorado or Leyden, Wisconsin also known for a post office operated from 1850 till 1903. Both were named after the Dutch town of Leiden. You can also find a Leyden in New York and in Illinois. However I would like to take a closer look at Leyden in Massachusetts, an agreeable quiet little town with a population of approx. 700 which is also named after the Dutch city.

Leyden Massachusetts is a *right to farm* community and when I asked Nicole Glabach, the local town clerk what this means, she explained that in the seventies all 50 states of the USA passed laws in order to protect farmers from being considered a nuisance by their neighbours.

In Leyden there are goat farms and dairy cow farms and when you look at the pictures there doesn't seem to be much difference between the Netherlands and this part of the USA !

USA

Netherlands

Today the largest industry in town is the maple sugar production. In March when the maple sugar season has come to a close Leyden celebrates with town suppers, such as *the sugar on snow supper* where locals gather to eat shepherd's pie made from locally produced meat (beef, lamb or goat) followed by *sugar on snow :* a local delicacy consisting of heated maple syrup drizzled immediately, without stirring over packed snow or shaved ice!

Tip : Check out the Leyden Life monthly newsletter for all the latest Leyden news.

Shepherd's Pie

Ovenschotel met gehakt en puree

Serves 4 p. or more

Preparation 15 minutes

Baking time 20 minutes

Shopping list

1 lb (500 g) ground beef

2 onions chopped

2 cups hot mashed potatoes

4 oz. or 120 g cream cheese, cubed

1 cup grated cheddar cheese

2 garlic cloves, minced

2 cups creamed corn

1 small can tomato puree

Pepper, salt, Worcester sauce

Ketjap Manis (sweet soy sauce)

Preparation

Preheat the oven to 375F/190C. Brown the meat in a skillet, add the onions, 1 minced clove of garlic and keep stirring. Once the onion is soft and tender add the tomato puree, Worcester sauce, Ketjap Manis and salt and pepper to taste. Allow it to simmer for approx. 5 minutes.

Meanwhile mix the mashed potatoes with the cream cheese, 1/2 cup of the grated cheese and 1 minced clove of garlic until smooth.

Place the cooked meat mixture on the bottom of a baking dish, adding 2 cups of corn and the mashed potatoes mix on top.

Sprinkle the remaining 1/2 cup of grated cheese on top of this mixture. Bake for 20 minutes until the cheese is melted and turned golden brown.

I always serve home-made apple sauce with it.

Enjoy !

Your personal notes

....

....

....

....

Leiden NL

Population : 123.000

Province : South Holland

Website : www.visitleiden.nl

A nickname of the town is "key city" referring to the coat of arms

Leiden has a long and rich history reaching back to the Middle Ages. During the 80 years' war (1568—1648) Leiden joined the Dutch resistance against the Spanish (see also Brielle page 16).

The recipe on the next page is inherited from the time of the Spanish occupation : due to the siege the local population was nearly dying of starvation. However on the 3rd October 1574 they succeeded in

forcing the Spanish troops out of the city. Due to this sudden retreat it is recounted that many of the cooking pots and pans still containing a type of stew containing carrots, onions and meat, were left behind. This liberation of the city is called *Leidens Ontzet* or the Relief of Leiden and is still celebrated each October. Then Leiden becomes one great festival for two consecutive days where the locals enjoy markets, concerts, parties, fireworks and traditional dishes. "Hutspot" has changed a little over time but is still a delicious dish today. As a reward for its heroic resistance Willem of Orange offered Leiden their university, which is now the oldest university of the Netherlands. Members of the Royal Family including Princess Beatrix and King Willem Alexander studied here.

Leiden is a fabulous city to visit with its many canals, monuments, shops and local history. Not forgetting the oldest theatre and university of the Netherlands, a variety of museums and many bars and terraces where you can sit and enjoy watching the

passers-by whilst experiencing the local Leiden vibes. Leiden was already famous during the Golden Age and is the birthplace of Rembrandt van Rijn as well as other famous painters such as Jan Steen. An inspiring city.

The Pilgrim museum is located in Leiden. Here you discover the link to Leyden in Massachusetts : in 1609 the Pilgrims were English protestant refugees who had fled to Leiden and could live there in peace

practising their own faith. The Pilgrim Fathers set sail in 1620 on the Speedwell and Mayflower to the USA and settled first in Plymouth Massachusetts and others later in Leyden. It is said that several American Presidents for example F.D. Roosevelt, Bush and Obama descend from these Pilgrim Fathers.

Hutspot met gehaktballen

Hotpot with meat balls

Serves 4 p.

Preparation 20 minutes

Cooking time 20 minutes hotpot
45 minutes meat balls

Shopping list

For the hotpot

2 lb (1 kg) floury potatoes

1 lb (500 g) winter carrots peeled and diced

1 lb (500 g) onions peeled and sliced

Salt, pepper, milk and if you like some crème fraiche

For the meat balls

1 lb (500 g) ground beef (mix of pork and beef)

1 egg

2 tablespoons Ketjap Manis (sweet soy sauce)

1/2 cup of breadcrumbs

1 sachet spice mix for meatloaf to taste

Butter and water

1 can of beef broth {16 oz.}

Preparation hotpot

Peel and quarter the potatoes, place them in a pan with water until just covered and add a little salt. Cover and bring to the boil. Add the carrots and put the onions on top. Bring to the boil once again, lower the heat, cover the pan and boil for approx. 20 minutes until the potatoes are cooked. Sieve and mash the potatoes, carrots and onions with a cup of milk, some butter and crème fraiche to taste, until you have the preferred consistency. Add salt and pepper to taste.

Preparation meat balls

Place the mix of beef and pork in a bowl together with the egg, sweet soy sauce, the breadcrumbs and the spice mix. Knead with hands to combine. Then form the mixture with wet hands into 4 or 5 meatballs. Melt butter in a pan until brown. Fry the meatballs for 5 minutes until browned on all sides. Stir water and beef broth into the pan, bring it all to a boil, reduce to a low heat and let it simmer for approx. 45 minutes until meatballs are cooked.

Enjoy !

Middleburg USA

Population : 800

State : Virginia

Website : www.middleburgva.gov

Christmas Parade

When you try to find Middleburg's link to the Netherlands, you may be disappointed ! Middleburg, Virginia is not named after Middelburg in the Netherlands but it was the middle or halfway stop between Alexandria and Winchester at the Ashby Gap Road, now part of Route 50.

Middleburg is a small country town approximately an hour's drive from Washington, DC. On route to Middleburg you will observe beautiful estates, wide open green spaces, vineyards, iron gates, horses in paddocks and beautiful dry stone walling. It has a strong resemblance to a typical English county landscape. Middelburg and its surrounding area is seen as horse and wine country. Whilst driving down the Zulla or Atoka road you can also admire this beautiful landscape and perhaps visit the Goose Creek Bridge.

Red Fox Inn and Tavern

On a cultural level, you can partake in a self guided walking tour provided by Middleburg's Visitor Centre. There are many art galleries and sites of interest to enjoy including the Civil War landmark.

The oldest building in town is the Red Fox Inn and Tavern. Many galleries, farms and stables have "fox" in their name referring to the fox hunting which takes place each year.

It is exceptional that this small town holds so many organized events, such as the famous Christmas Parade, an International Classical Music Festival and a renowned Film Festival which bring many stars and tourists to town (such as Jacqueline Kennedy—former first lady—in days gone by) .

Photo's courtesy of Vincent Bataoël

Meatloaf with mushrooms

Gehaktbrood met champignons

Serves 6 p.

Preparation 15 minutes

Cooking time 60 minutes

Shopping list

1 lb (500 g) ground beef

2 slices of wheat meal loaf (make bread crumbs yourself with food processor)

3,5 oz. (approx. 12 rashers) bacon

1/2 lb (250 g) sliced mushrooms

1 tablespoon Dijon mustard

1/4 cup red wine (60 ml)

1 egg

3 tablespoons butter (50 g)

thyme, sage

1 onion finely chopped

1 crushed garlic clove

1/2 sachet spice mix for meatloaf

Loaf or cake tin

Preparation

Fry the minced onion and garlic with a knob of butter in a large pan until soft and golden. Add thyme, sage and the mushrooms, fry together with onion and garlic. Add the red wine and allow to simmer for several minutes and then lower the heat.

Mix the meat in a bowl with the bread crumbs, the egg, mustard and the half sachet of meatloaf spice mix. Add the onion-mushroom mixture until thoroughly mixed.

Preheat the oven to 350F /170C.

Line the loaf tin with slightly overlapping strips of bacon and let them hang over the edge. Add the meat mixture in the loaf tin and cover it with the overhanging bacon.

Place the loaf tin in the oven for at least one hour. Remove from the oven, let it rest for 10 minutes then slice for serving.

Enjoy !

This is my mum's recipe for meatloaf. Of course one can prepare meatloaf in a variety of ways using all left overs from your weekend dishes. Or incorporating the meat with a packet of your favourite vegetable soup mix, as my friend Charline does, but meatloaf with mushrooms was my mum's favourite !

Middelburg NL

Population : 39.500

Province : Zeeland

Website : www.middelburg.nl

City Hall of Middelburg

Middelburg is a captivating city and also the capital of the Dutch province of Zeeland. Whilst strolling down the avenue from the station towards the centre of this small town you can admire their numerous monuments. During the Golden Age Middelburg was seen as a wealthy harbour city and is still considered so today. The monuments that were destroyed during the Second World War have been remarkably well restored. Pay a visit to both their gothic city hall and to the Middelburg Abbey which still has remnants that were built in the 11th century by the Flemish Norbertine monks. In 1574 after the Siege of Middelburg monastic life came to an end and the commoners swore faith to William of Orange. William took a residence at the Abbey, an apartment of which the royal family has made use of in the past.

Although Middleburg USA has no link to the Netherlands, Middelburg in the Netherlands does however have a link to the USA :

Each year the Roosevelt Four Freedoms awards is presented to men, women or organisations whose achievements have demonstrated a commitment to Franklin D. Roosevelt's four Freedoms: freedom of speech and expression, freedom of worship, freedom from want and freedom from fear. Presentation of the Four Freedoms Awards is a tradition begun by the Franklin and Eleanor Roosevelt Institute in New York in 1950. Roosevelt's ancestors came from Oud-Vossemeer, a village in Zeeland (page 52). Since 1982, the centennial of President Roosevelt's birth and bicentennial of diplomatic relations between the USA and the Netherlands, the presentation has been organised internationally in collaboration with the Roosevelt Foundation in Zeeland. The Awards are presented in Middelburg in even years (often in the presence of members of the Royal Family) and in New York in odd years. (www.fourfreedoms.nl).

Examples of Laureates :

Desmond Tutu, Angela Merkel, Human Rights Watch, Malala, Red Cross and many more...

Fun Dutch (Food) Fact:

Zeeuwse bolus : the name comes from the Yiddish language of Portuguese Jewish people that came to Middelburg in the 17th century. "Bole" meant delicate pastry. Now it sometimes is associated with poo because of the shape !

Zeeuwse bolus

Cinnamon rolls from Zeeland

For 15 cinnamon rolls

Preparation 30 minutes

Rising time (dough) 1 hour

Baking time 7-8 minutes

Shopping list

3,5 cups (500 g) of all purpose flour

1 tablespoon of caster sugar (15 g)

1 egg, room temperature

0,5 teaspoon of salt (10 g)

1 cube of fresh yeast (1,5 oz. or 42 g)

1 cup of water (200 ml)

1/4 cup of lukewarm milk (60 ml)

5 tablespoons of butter, room temperature

2 cups of dark brown sugar (400 g)

1 tablespoon of cinnamon

Preparation

Mix the flour, caster sugar, salt and egg together. Dissolve the yeast in the lukewarm milk. Add this to the flour mixture and knead the dough for 6 minutes by hand or in a food processor. Add the butter during the last 4 minutes of the kneading process. Then continue to knead for a further 8 minutes. Let it rest for 5 minutes.

Mix the brown sugar and cinnamon and divide this mixture on a large plate or cutting board.

Knead the dough once more shortly and divide into small balls of approx. 2,5 oz. (70 g). Roll out into ropes of about 10 inches (25 cm). Cover with a few drops of water and roll them in the sugar/cinnamon mixture until completely covered.. Take one end of the rope and roll it around itself. Tuck the end underneath the "bolus" and place them on a sheet of parchment paper on a baking sheet. Leave enough space for them to expand and cover with foil and allow them to rise for 1 hour at a warm place. After 50 minutes : preheat the oven at 450F/225C.

Bake the "bolussen" for 7-8 minutes until puffy, sticky and fully baked.

Eat them while still slightly warm and spread a little butter on the bottom as an extra treat : delicious !

Your personal notes

....

....

....

....

Nassau Village USA

Population : 1600

State : New York

Website : www.nassau12123.com

Nassau is a village located in the Town of Nassau in Rensselaer County, in the state of New York. History does not explain why this village - originally known as Union Village and Schermerhorn's Village (Schermerhorn : also a village in the Netherlands) - was incorporated in 1819 and became known as Nassau Village. No doubt its roots can be found somewhere in the Dutch colonial period.

Nassau village has a charming website (see above) and publishes a popular monthly newsletter "The Village Green". In 2019 the Village of Nassau will celebrate its bicentenary when a series of festivities will take place !

A walking tour of Nassau is posted on their website and as you read this brief guide to the buildings and history of the Nassau Village you cannot fail to notice that the Dutch influence is still abundant and many Dutch names still appear : for example the Van Valkenburgh Store 1786 and the Lucas Vandenberg-Huested House 1870's.

One remarkable anecdote involves the Nassau House Hotel where, as the story goes, Martin Van Buren often went for evening dinners in the 1840's. Martin van Buren was born on 5th December 1782 in Kinderhook New York and was the descendant of Dutch settlers. He became the 8th President of the United States of America and was the founder of the Democratic Party. His nickname was the Red Fox of Kinderhook. Amusingly King Willem Alexander of Oranje Nassau (the current Dutch monarch) participated at the Eleven cities tour (see page 20) using the alias W.A. van Buren (!)

Each year several community events are organized such as the Nassaufest in September providing carnival games for the kids, musical entertainment, fun for the whole family and food and drinks at a reasonable price (perhaps even coleslaw is served - for the recipe see next page).

Nassau House Hotel. Photos courtesy of Mr. Kurt Vincent

Coleslaw

Koolsla

The origin of coleslaw is the Dutch word Kool (cabbage) and Sla (salad)

Serves 4 p.

Preparation 15 minutes

Resting time in fridge 1 hour

Shopping list

For the salad

4 cups or 400 g white cabbage

1,5 cup or 150 g of grated carrots (julienne)

0,5 cup granulated sugar (100 g)

0,25 cup kosher salt (75g)

For the dressing :

5 tablespoons mayonnaise

1 tablespoon cider vinegar

6 drops Worcestershire sauce

2 tablespoons tomato ketchup

1 teaspoon celery salt

1 tablespoon granulated sugar

1 teaspoon freshly ground black pepper

3 to 4 spring onions

4 tablespoons fresh chopped or frozen parsley leaves

Preparation

Place the sliced white cabbage and grated carrots into a salad spinner and sprinkle with the sugar and kosher salt. Toss the ingredients and let them rest for 5 minutes allowing the moisture to drain from the cabbage.

In the meantime you can make a start on the dressing : mix all ingredients for the dressing into a medium sized bowl. A spicy result is preferred.

Rinse the cabbage and carrots mixture very thorough with cold water. Spin the ingredients in the salad spinner again and place them in a large bowl.

Pour the dressing over the coleslaw and toss the ingredients thoroughly. Season with salt and pepper to taste.

Cover the bowl and refrigerate for 1 hour before serving.

This delicious creamy coleslaw goes very well with a hamburger in a bun or as a side-dish to your barbecue.

Baarle—Nassau NL

Population : 6.585

Province : Noord Brabant

Website : www.baarle-nassau.nl

The most peculiar village in the world is how the tourist office in Baarle—Nassau describes itself. Why ? Because Baarle—Nassau is an enclave of the larger village Baarle where 30 pieces of Belgian and Dutch lands are connected to each other by complicated borders, like a puzzle.

The village has two of everything (Belgian and Dutch) : 2 community councils, 2 mayors, 2 police forces, even 2 post offices. The registered house numbers are both Belgian and Dutch, the traffic signs are different and so much more !

You may cross the Dutch/Belgian borders several times without your knowledge whilst walking in these attractive streets. The pavements indicate the borders by means of lettered paving tiles either NL (Netherlands) or B (Belgium).

Baarle—Nassau is a very lively village with many terraces, restaurants and shops.

Fun Dutch (Food) Fact:

The traditional Brabant Sausage Roll has been on the UNESCO list of immaterial cultural heritage since 2016! Nowadays you can buy and eat them daily, however in the old days they were eaten predominantly after the night mass at Christmas, during Carnival and during the annual Fair.

Brabants worstenbrood

Sausage rolls from Brabant

This is the recipe from my friend Lian's mother

For 14 sausage rolls

Preparation 30 minutes

Rising time (dough) 1 hour

Baking time 15 to 20 minutes

Shopping list

1 lb all purpose flour (500 g)

2 tablespoons lard (45 g)

1 cup of lukewarm milk (200 ml)

1 cube of fresh yeast (1,5 oz. or 42 g)

1/2 tablespoon salt

1/2 tablespoon sugar

2 eggs

1 lb (500 g) ground beef (preferably half beef, half pork) seasoned

1/2 cup breadcrumbs

Preparation

Dissolve the yeast in lukewarm milk. Put the flour, lard, yeast, sugar, salt and milk together and knead.

Let it rise for 1 hour.

Meanwhile knead the ground beef with pepper, salt, 1 egg and the breadcrumbs. Roll the beef into sausages (see photo's). After one hour divide the dough into approx. 14 pieces. Roll out the dough.

Preheat the oven to 430F/220C.

Roll the sausage into a bowl of flower ensuring a slightly covered surface and place it on the dough. First fold the short sides, then fold the long side over the short sides. It has to be wrapped quite tightly. Brush the sausages with beaten egg or alternatively with a little milk.

Bake in the oven for 15 to 20 minutes until golden. Remove the rolls and let them rest on a baking rack.

Of course you can change the filling of the roll to taste, even a veggie roll is possible but these are the original sausage rolls from the Dutch province Brabant and surely the best you have ever tasted !

Your personal notes

....

....

....

....

Schenectady USA

Motto : "The city that lights and hauls the world"

Population : 66.000

State : New York

Website : www.cityofschenectady.com

Arrival of Goos Terschegget in Schenectady
Courtesy of Edith Terschegget

The city of Schenectady thanks its name to the first inhabitants of the region : the Mohawk. They called it "skahnéhtati" which means "beyond the pines".

This settlement was founded by Arendt van Curler (1619-1667 who originated from Nijkerk—page 40—in the Netherlands) a Dutchman who immigrated to the USA together with his nephew Kiliaen van Rensselaer. More than 300 years later in 1984, another descendant from Nijkerk and former alderman, Goos Terschegget sailed solo in 41 days from the Netherlands to Schenectady as part of a single-handed cross-Atlantic sailing race. A group of fellow-townsmen flew in especially to celebrate this achievement and to welcome him to Schenectady.

A tradition was born.

Since then a bi-annual adult exchange has taken place where one year residents hailing from Nijkerk visit Schenectady and the following year a reciprocate trip involving a group from Schenectady are received in Nijkerk. In recent years a youth exchange has been added to the agenda making this an annual tradition. The two cities have become sister cities and all citizens of Nijkerk have become honorary citizens of the City of Schenectady. You can read more about this historical bond at the following websites :

Www.schenectadynijkerk.org

Www.nijkerk-schenectady.nl

Local interest information can also be found on www.historicstockade.com where you are able to read more about popular places to visit in Schenectady. Historic Stockade for example is a residential neighbourhood that has buildings dating back to the early 1700s.

How did the motto of Schenectady come into being? The motto is a reference to the two most important businesses in the city : the Edison Electric Company, also known as General Electric and the American Locomotive Company (ALCO).

Dutch doughnuts and Apple fritters

Oliebollen en appelbeignets : New Year's eve treat

Quantity approx. 25 Dutch doughnuts and 15 apple fritters

Preparation 30 minutes

Dough rise 45 minutes

Frying time 3 to 4 minutes per pan

Shopping list

For the Dutch doughnuts

2 cups of all purpose flour (500 g)
2 cups of lukewarm milk (400 ml)
2 tablespoons of active dry yeast (40 g)
2 tablespoons of soft butter (40 g)
2 eggs
Pinch of salt

For the Apple fritters

1 cup of self raising flour (250 g)
2 eggs
1 cup of milk (200 ml)
4 tart apples (Granny Smith or Jonagold)
1 teaspoon of cinnamon

Frying pan
1 to 2 litres of sunflower oil
Icing sugar

Preparation Dutch doughnuts

Dissolve the yeast in the lukewarm milk. Stir flour, pinch of salt, the milk with yeast, 2 eggs and the butter until smooth. Cover the dough with cling film and place it in a warm, draught-free area for 45 minutes by which time the dough should have doubled in size.

Heat the sunflower oil in a deep pan up to 360F/190C. Using 2 tablespoons to form a dough ball gently drop the doughnut in the hot oil for approx. 4 minutes. Use a slotted spoon to turn the balls and fry until golden brown on both sides. Place the doughnuts on absorbent kitchen roll in order to soak up any excess grease. Add a sprinkling of icing sugar for the finishing touch !

Preparation Apple fritters.

Mix together the flour, eggs, milk and a pinch of salt. Peel and de-core the apples. Slice in rings, a little less than 1/2 inch (1 cm) thick. Place the slices in the batter and coat them on both sides. Gently drop 4 to 5 slices carefully into the hot oil (360F/190C)). Turn over when golden brown and in approx. 4 minutes they should be perfect. Leave to drain on absorbent kitchen roll. Sprinkle with icing sugar and a little cinnamon.

Happy New Year !

Tips

Add raisins or currants to the unrisen dough to make raisin doughnuts.

Alternative ingredients to apple are banana or pineapple which also make delicious fritters.

Nijkerk NL

Population : 41.000

Province : Gelderland

Website : www.nijkerk.eu

Nijkerk is a historic city and its name means "New Church". Since 1221 the church has been destroyed several times due to fire or war. The most recent Great Church was rebuilt in the 18th century. This small city of Nijkerk has had many notable residents including Christiaan Eijkman, a Nobel prize winner in 1929 in the field of Physiology or Medicine (for the discovery of certain vitamins). Kiliaen van Rensselaer—whose name is still familiar in New York state due to Rensselaer city in Rensselaer County— must also be included in this list having had his roots in Nijkerk. The Van Rensselaer family has an imposing family tombstone within the Great Church.

However in regard to this book Arendt van Curler as founder of Schenectady is seen as the most important notable resident of Nijkerk. As referred earlier Nijkerk and Schenectady have maintained close bonds over the centuries. The Foundation Nijkerk-Schenectady preserves and promotes this relationship and has established the "Friends of the Foundation" society. Their membership subscription is used to fund the youth exchanges and other foundation activities, for example the annual potluck dinner organised for friends of the foundation.

In my search for an appropriate recipe for the Schenectady page I received a cookbook from Edith Terschegget, president of the Foundation Nijkerk-Schenectady and daughter of Goos Terschegget (page 38) —named "Kiss the Cook". It was published in 1984 by The Women's League First Reformed Church of Schenectady, New York and is full of original recipes of Schenectady locals and several sourced from European descendants such as Ruth E.

George's Swedish Apple Pie, Judy Bierbaum's French Coq au Vin, Connie Blair's Breast of Chicken Italiano and Dutch recipes including Millie Casey's Jan Hagel Cookies and Pat Dijkstra's Dutch pancakes.

My final choice fell on the Dutch New Year's eve treat because if you make this easy recipe you are sure to get kissed ! (page 39)

Fun Dutch Fact:

In the Netherlands there are more bicycles than people : around 23 million bikes for 17 million people and as a result cycling in the Netherlands is the safest in the world thanks to 35.000 km cycle lanes.

Stimpstamp met karnemelksesaus

Endive stew with buttermilk sauce

Serves 4 p.

Preparation 15 minutes

Cooking time 20 minutes

Shopping list

2 lbs (1 kg) potatoes
1 lbs (500 g) curly endive cut into
small strips
Butter and milk
Pepper and salt

For the sauce

7 oz. (200 g) diced bacon
1 tablespoon butter
1 tablespoon all purpose flour
1 cup of buttermilk (200 ml)
A pinch of nutmeg
Salt & pepper

Preparation

Peel the potatoes and cut them into 4 or 8 wedges depending on the size. Cover the potatoes in water and bring them to a boil. Add a pinch of salt, lower the heat and allow them to simmer for about 20 minutes.

Drain the water and mash the potatoes with butter and milk until you have a smooth puree. Add the raw endive strips, mix well together and add salt and pepper to taste.

Buttermilk sauce

Gently fry the diced bacon in the butter. Then add the flour and while stirring pour in the buttermilk. Stir until you have a smooth sauce. Add a little nutmeg, fresh salt and pepper and serve it together with the endive stew.

It looks very easy—and it is ! The smoothness of the potatoes and the crunch of the endive stew together with the salty sauce will surprise you....

Enjoy !

Your personal notes

....

....

....

....

Orange City USA

Population : 6000

State : Iowa

Website : orangecityiowa.com

All photos courtesy of Orange City Chamber of Commerce

Orange City in Iowa is named after Prince William III of Orange - ancestor to the current Dutch monarch William—Alexander, who is not only known as King of the Netherlands but also as Prince of Orange. Many of the inhabitants of Orange City have Dutch roots.

This becomes obvious whilst walking from the entrance of Northwestern College on the southern side of the town towards Windmill Park. You will see windmills, flowers and Dutch facades and stepped gables which adorn many of the buildings.

The Chamber of Commerce is established in a windmill and if you pay a visit to the Stadscentrum for example, you can still find clog or wooden shoe making equipment.

Each year during the third weekend of May there is a Tulip Festival which attracts many local residents as well as those of the neighbouring towns.

Folk still enjoy eating poffertjes (small pancakes), oliebollen (see recipe page 39) and stroopwafels (syrup waffles) ! I was delighted to receive the recipe of the renowned and delicious Amsterdam roast, however it was impossible to prepare this in the Netherlands, as it requires buying an "Amsterdam Roast" from Woudstra's Meat Market — a well-known butcher in Orange City. You can find an interesting short film about the history of this store on You Tube should you want to know more about it.

I also found a short film on You Tube regarding The Dutch bakery in Orange City which shows you the preparation of the almond patties they bake every Tulip Festival. As a working bakery they will prepare their own dough of course, but I can give you my own quick version of almond patties on the next page. They are so easy to make !

Almond patties

Amandelbroodjes

Serves 10 large patties or 30 smaller ones

Preparation 20 minutes

Baking time 20 minutes

Shopping list

1 parcel of frozen puff pastry (10 squares)

1 large or medium egg

1 packet of almond paste (10 oz. or 300 g)

1/2 cup of sugar (100 g)

Preparation

Preheat the oven to 390F/200C. Thaw the puff pastry (5 minutes). Beat the egg with a fork and mix 3/4 of the egg through the almond paste until you have a smooth, sticky substance.

Place the sugar (raw sugar or coarse sugar for the best result) on a small plate.

Place a small roll of almond paste (+/- 1 ounce or 30 grams) onto each square of puff pastry. Wet the edges of the puff pastry with a little water. Roll up the puff pastry making sure all the almond paste is covered. If you prefer the small patties : cut the roll in 3 equal parts. Brush a little of the remaining egg (possibly mixed with a little milk) on the top of the patty and dip it into the raw sugar.

Place the patties on a baking sheet and bake them in the oven for about 20 minutes until golden.

Tip : if you have any puff pastry in the freezer and a packet of almond paste in your pantry, you will always have a quick treat for unexpected guests.

Your personal notes

....

....

....

....

Oranje NL

Population : 140

Province : Drenthe

Website : www.middendrenthe.nl

Oranje is located in the province Drenthe and in the 19th century the province was predominately covered by moorland. Once cultivation of the moorland started around 1850, the investors of the time chose to dig a canal which could transport the peat off the moors. This canal was named the Oranje canal at the official opening in the presence of King Willem III (of Oranje Nassau). Nowadays the canal is approximately 45 kilometres long (27 miles). Agricultural land replaced the moors due to the removal of the peat and this land became especially useful to potato farmers. A couple of farmers settled here and founded a

potato flour factory. The factory required a workforce, houses were built, shops opened and at one time there even was a school. The village Oranje was born. Nowadays this canal village has a population of around 140 and is so small that it doesn't even have street names !

The potato flour factory has always played an important role in the region, initially as a factory for the workers, later as a covered kindergarten with resort and later still as a temporary accommodation for some 700 refugees.

The Midden-Drenthe tourist information office can provide you with all you need to know about the area and you can stroll around and enjoy all Oranje, Oranjekanaal and its countryside has to offer. Oranje is situated between two important national parks and their booklet will tell you not only about its history but also about its rich flora and fauna.

"Diependal" which is located nearby Oranje and although offering no access for visitors in order to maintain the peace and quiet of the area, does however have a birdwatch hide in the centre of the wetland nature reserve which can be reached by means of an underground tunnel. If you want to discover this lovely little village : there are some bed and breakfasts in the neighbourhood.

King Willem III van Oranje Nassau

I went to visit Oranje on King's Day when the whole country turns orange. I saw this lovely orange car in Oranje and in the background the old potato flour factory.

King Willem-Alexander van Oranje Nassau (and his wife Queen Maxima)

Kniepertjes

Old and New Year's waffles from Drenthe

Makes 60 to 70 waffles

Preparation 10 minutes
(if possible 1 night resting time)

Baking time 1,5 minute for each waffle

Shopping list

1 lb all purpose flour (500 g)

1 stick butter (125 g)

2 cups caster sugar (375 g)

3 eggs

1 sachet vanilla sugar

3 tablespoons lukewarm water

2 tablespoons gin (if available—for extra crispy waffles)

1 pinch of salt

Flat waffle iron / ice cream cone maker or pizzelle.

Whipped cream

Preparation

Melt the butter and allow it to cool down a little. Mix the flour, the caster sugar and the vanilla sugar and stir in the melted butter until you have a crumbly dough. Add a pinch of salt. Knead the eggs one at a time through the dough. Add the water and gin until dough is of consistent texture. If you have the time, let it rest for 24 hours in the fridge.

Remove the dough from the fridge and roll into small balls, about the size of a soup ball. Put the ball in the waffle iron, flatten it and bake for about 1,5 minute until golden brown. If you want to make the rolled up version : remove the waffle of the iron and immediately roll it around the handle of a wooden spoon. The waffles become crispy once they have cooled on a plate (don't make a pile as they will not cool down)

Really easy to make and delicious !

These "kniepertjes" are a specialty in Oranje and the province Drenthe and are baked at the end of each year : the flat waffles symbolize the Old Year where all the events have been revealed and the rolled ones symbolize the New Year , still a mystery of the events yet to come. Often served filled with whipped cream.

Rotterdam USA

Slogan : *Rotterdam is a nice place to live*

Population : 29.000

State : New York

Website : www.rotterdamny.org

Rotterdam, NY— which became a Dutch settlement in the 17th century—used to be a part of Schenectady city. It was named after Rotterdam in the Netherlands and since World War II (when the old world Rotterdam was heavily bombed and almost completely destroyed) Rotterdam NY adopted the seal of the old Rotterdam.

After World War II Queen Wilhelmina of the Netherlands granted the motto "Stronger Through Effort" to be added to the seal. Both cities now use the same seal and motto.

Memorial Monument that is in the front of the Town Hall
Courtesy of the *Supervisor's Office Town of Rotterdam*

The oldest house still standing in Rotterdam and example of early Dutch American architecture, is the Jan Mabee House built by Jan Pieterse Mabee around 1705. It has been passed on from generation to generation until the latest family proprietor, Mr. George Franchere, donated the Mabee farm to the Schenectady County Historical Society. You are still able to visit the farm as it has been developed into a museum and educational centre for the community. For more interesting facts take a glance at : "gremsdoolittlelibrary.blogspot.com".

Jan Mabee House

From the collection of the Schenectady County Historical Society

As Rotterdam NY is often referred to by its nickname of New Italy (due to many inhabitants with Italian roots) take a look on the next page for my own tomato pasta sauce recipe

Sauce Bolognese

Bolognese saus

Serves 4—6 p.

Preparation 30 minutes

Cooking time approx. 2 hours

Shopping list

1 tablespoon of butter

2 tablespoons of olive oil

2 onions chopped

3 cloves garlic finely chopped

2 carrots trimmed and finely chopped

2 celery sticks finely chopped

1 lb (500 g) ground beef

4 slices of bacon chopped

Salt, pepper

1 little bag Italian herbs (11 g)

2 x (14 oz. or 400 g) can of diced tomatoes with juice

1 small can of tomato puree

1 cup of red wine

2 teaspoons of granulated sugar

Preparation

Melt the butter and heat the olive oil together in a casserole pan and fry the onion and garlic until soft.

Add the carrots and celery to the pan and fry again for approx. 4 minutes. Add the ground beef, the chopped bacon and cook until the meat is evenly brown.

Add salt, pepper, the Italian herbs and reduce to medium heat until most of the moisture is evaporated.

Then add the tomatoes with juice, tomato puree, the wine and let everything simmer gently for about 2 hours until you have a thick rich sauce. Stir from time to time and season to taste.

Serve with spaghetti and grated parmesan cheese.

Enjoy !

Your personal notes

....

....

....

....

Rotterdam NL

Population : 610.386

Province : Zuid Holland

Website : https://en.rotterdam.info

What can I tell you about Rotterdam? Rotterdam has so many beautiful spots that it is impossible to show them all to you. Take for example the Cube Houses designed by the architect Piet Blom, the Euromast which provides you with an unparalleled view of the city, the Old or Pilgrim Father's Church which was a haven for the Pilgrim Fathers on their way to America many centuries ago and of course there is the SS Rotterdam, the biggest ocean steamer ever built in the Netherlands. It is the former flag ship of the Holland – America Line. Just a selection of the many memorable places you must be sure to visit.

I have decided to introduce to you one of Rotterdam's latest highlight : the Markthal or food hall. This is the first covered market in the Netherlands. It includes an enormous market floor under an arch of apartments. The building was designed by the architects of MVRDV. The shape, the colourful interior and the height turn Markthal into a spectacle that you cannot find anywhere in the world. Wandering around the 100 fresh food stands, you can look up and admire the artwork known as the "Horn of Plenty" by Arno Coenen and Iris Roskam on the ceiling. In the background you can also see St. Laurens Church. The artists' aim was to recreate the feeling you may have had whilst reading Alice in Wonderland. The ceiling shows illustrations of huge fruit and vegetables, insects and fish.

This picture shows the outside of the Markthal with an impression of the inside ceiling with St. Laurens Church.

Boerenkoolstamppot met worst

Kale hash with sausage

Serves 4 p.

Preparation 10 minutes

Cooking time 20 minutes

Shopping list

2 lbs (1 kg) potatoes

1 lb (500 g) kale (pre sliced)

1 pinch salt

1 pinch pepper

1 or 2 smoked sausages
(rookworst) or equivalent

1 oz. (100 g) bacon

1/2 cup milk (100 ml)

3 tablespoons butter

Sour cream (optional)

Preparation

Peel and dice the potatoes.

If you are unable to purchase pre sliced kale, you clean, trim and slice a whole kale.

Place the washed potatoes, sliced kale, a pinch of salt and just enough water to cover all the ingredients in a large pan.

Cover and boil gently for approx. 20 minutes.

Meanwhile prepare the smoked sausage according to instructions on the bag (takes about the same time : 20 minutes)

Fry the bacon until crispy.

Drain the vegetables and mash them together whilst adding milk and butter (and some sour cream if you like)

Stir in the hot smoked sausage, add salt and pepper to taste and serve.

Tip : in order to give the kale hash the same taste as that from the province Brabant add some drops of vinegar.

Zeeland USA

Population : 6000

State : Michigan

Website : www.ci.zeeland.mi.us

Slogan : "Feel the Zeel"

Founder of Zeeland was Jannes van de Luyster, an elder born in 1789 in Cadzand, in the Dutch province of Zeeland. In early 1847 Jannes van de Luyster decided to sell his property and leave with his family for America. His decision was based predominantly on economic and religious reasons. De Luyster was no fortune seeker but a serious and religious man who was looking for a place where he might experience the religious freedom of expression he so craved. These Dutch Reformed separatists travelled as an organized religious community of approximately 400 worshippers. Jannes van de Luyster, a philanthropist, covered the cost of the trip for 77 of the voyagers (www.gereformeerdekerken.info) and thus helped many poor families.

Dutch woonerf gathering place in downtown Zeeland

Zeeland has expanded and flourished since those early days. Supplementary to the population of approx. 6000, a further 12.000 workers flock to the city each day. Certain vestiges of the city's Dutch heritage still remain, which can be found in the exhibits at the Zeeland Museum/the Dekker House and this heritage can also be found in a downtown Kings Day celebration featuring the local high school Dutch dancers dressed in the traditional costumes of all the Dutch provinces who go on the dance at the Tulip Festival in neighbouring town of Holland (page 22).

Each year at the 5th of December the museum celebrates *Sinterklaas (Saint Nicholas)* with small children being able to tell their wishes to the Good Holy Man. The Zeeland Bakery makes several favourite Dutch treats, such as *banketstaaf, saucijzenbroodjes, speculaas* and *krakelingen. Saucijzenbroodjes* are also made for charity on a monthly basis : they are sold to support local and world mission projects run by a Zeeland church group.

Aerial view of the Dekker House and Zeeland Historical Museum

In Zeeland there is an array of local festivals including the popular criterium bike race (see also Zeeland Netherlands), a pumpkin fest, summer concerts and much, much more. The Dutch-American Heritage dinner is celebrated each year in November with a wonderful traditional Dutch dinner and famous special guest speakers like for example Dr. Jan Pol, the veterinarian or Vincent Willem van Gogh just to name some.

Zeeland's residents are proud of their community due to its heritage of honest work, cleanliness, friendly relationships and care for others, reflecting the principles upon which the city was founded by Van de Luyster and his church community.

Courtesy Dorothy Voss and Zeeland Historical Society (www.zeelandhistory.org)

"Welkom" by Zeeland High School Dutch dancers

Pretzels

Krakelingen

For approx. 14 pretzels

Preparation 10 minutes

Baking time 25 minutes

Shopping list

4 slices of frozen puff pastry

1 egg yolk

3 tablespoons cream or milk

1/4 cup (50 g) cane sugar

1 teaspoon cinnamon

Preparation

Preheat the oven to 360F /180C. Thaw the puff pastry (5 minutes). Stack the 4 slices of puff pastry and roll them until you have a square slice of approx. twice the original size.

Cut the pastry in long stripes of about 1/2 inch (1,5 cm) wide.

Cover the baking try with baking paper. Form the stripes into pretzels by making half a circle on the baking tray and folding in the two ends crosswise. Press the ends gently.

Mix the egg yolk with the cream or milk and brush the top of the pretzels. Mix the cane sugar with the cinnamon and sprinkle on top.

For the best result : leave them to rest for 10 minutes. Bake the pretzels until golden brown in approx. 25 minutes.

The saucijzenbroodjes are called Pig-in-the-blanket in the Zeeland Bakery : a real neat name ! You will find the recipe of these sausage rolls on page 37. In the Netherlands a sausage roll is made with normal short-crust dough, a saucijzenbroodje is a "pig-in-the-blanket" but the blanket is puff pastry. You should try it once, this is really nice too.

Banket (staaf) = almond patties—see for the recipe page 43

Banketstaaf and pigs-in-the-blanket from the Zeeland Bakery on a Dutch plate owned by Dorothy Voss

Zeeland NL

Population : 382.000

Province : Zeeland

Website : www.zeeland.nl
www.vvvzeeland.nl

Zeeland—land in Sea—is a province on the west coast of the Netherlands incorporating many islands and beaches. In fact, the coastline meanders 650 km along dikes, dunes and beaches and as such is regarded as a much loved recreational spot for many tourists.

As in Zeeland USA, a Zeeland bicycle tour is organized annually and this Tacx Pro Classic of 130 km passes through all the highlights of the isles Walcheren, Schouwen-Duiveland and North and South Beveland. One of these famous features is Neeltje Jans, a family and educational park where you can learn all about the famous Delta Works—built after the flood catastrophe in 1953 to prevent that this ever reoccurring. (www.neeltjejans.nl).

Courtesy beeldenbank.laatzeelandzien.nl—a peloton cyclists at the storm surge barrier. Photo by Felice Buonadonna.

Beach in Vlissingen

These islanders and Zeeland locals often make use of mussels, oysters, lobster and cockles in their kitchen. Some famous sweet delicacies from Zeeland include cinnamon rolls (page 33) and "boterbabbelaars", see recipe on next page.

Middelburg is the province's capital (see page 32). Vlissingen is a harbour on the Westerschelde (river), and it is here that you will find the longest seaside boulevard of the Netherlands, a place where you can spend the afternoon just watching the ships sail by. On one side of this boulevard you will find a statue of the famous sea hero Michiel de Ruyter. If you are interested in maritime history take the time and visit the Muzeeum.

In 1965 the Zeelandbridge was completed. A 5022 m. (approx. 3 miles) bridge connecting the isles of Noord Beveland and Schouwen– Duiveland. At that time the longest bridge in Europe.

Veere

Zeeuwse Boterbabbelaars

Butterscotch from Zeeland

For approx. 30 candies

Preparation 5 minutes

Cooking time 10 minutes

Shopping list

1 cup sugar (250 g)
1 teaspoon water (5 ml)
1 tablespoon vinegar (15 ml)
1 tablespoon dairy butter (15 g)
Pinch of salt
Silicone baking mat

Preparation

Place all the ingredients in a saucepan on medium heat. Once the butter is melted give it one good stir to ensure that everything is well mixed. Do not stir again and heat the mixture to 300-320F/150-160 C. If you do not own a thermometer : the mixture is ready if it hardens immediately when dropped in cold water.

Poor the mixture on a silicone baking mat and keep it moving. When it begins to harden, create nice long strands of the still hot mixture. Tip : put silicone gloves on to protect you from the heat and the sticky mixture. Cut the strands into the size of candy pieces you prefer. Once cooled, place the butterscotch in a tin, possibly with a little powdered sugar to prevent from sticking to each other.

Fun Dutch Fact:

The Dutch are the world experts on controlling water from sea and rivers and sometimes it is said that the Dutch are the only people in the world to conquer land without fighting any war....

Zwolle USA

Tamale Capital of the World

Population : 1.984

State : Louisiana

Website : www.zwollela.net

Zwolle in Louisiana is situated along the Kansas City Southern railway. This was the first railroad from the North to the South in the USA (instead of from the East to the West) and was the personal vision of the founder, Arthur Stilwell (1859-1928) who understood the necessity of reliable transportation from the rich south (corn, wheat, coal, cattle, rye, lead, zinc etc.) to their sale markets in the north.

After the economic depression in 1896 Arthur Stillwell ran short of funds and approached Jan de Goeijen for assistance. De Goeijen was a wealthy Dutchman born in Zwolle (1861), coffee trader and owner of tea plantations, whom he had met on one of his travels on the liner s.s. Amsterdam. He convinced De Goeijen to invest in the railroad and they established their headquarters in "Hurray City" Arkansas which was eventually renamed "De Queen" after De Goeijen as De Goeijen's name was too difficult to pronounce in English and sounded like "De Queen".

To tell the truth the literal translation of De Goeijen is : *The good one*. In De Queen there still is a statue of De Goeijen to be found.

The railway started in Kansas City, Arkansas and was completed in 1897 in Port Arthur, Texas. This town was named after Arthur Stilwell however several towns situated alongside the railroad were related to De Goeijen e.g. :

Mena, Arkansas : Mena was an affectionate name for De Goeijens wife Folmina De Goeijen Janssen

DeRidder, Louisiana : family name of his sister-in-law

Amsterdam, Missouri : location of his firm

Zwolle, Louisiana : place of birth of De Goeijen

The first inhabitants of the land that was to become Zwolle were the native Americans who were on friendly terms with the French and Spanish newcomers who arrived in the 18th century. They intermarried and today most of the people in Zwolle are from either French-native American or Spanish-native American descent. In order to celebrate these roots the annual Zwolle Tamale Festival takes place during the second weekend of October. The local delicacy known as tamales have been made in the area since the early 1700s and nowadays Zwolle has become the Tamale Capital of the World !

Kansas City Southern Railway

Tamales

From the Zwolle Tamale Festival

For approx. 20 tamales

Preparation 1 afternoon

Steaming time 60 minutes

Shopping list

1/2 box (16 oz. or 0,5 l) chicken broth

1 cup drained corn kernels

2 cups (280 g) masa harina

1 teaspoon salt

1 teaspoon baking powder

1/4 cup (50 g) lard, chilled

2 dozen dried corn husks

1 medium onion, chopped

3 cloves garlic, crushed

1 lb (500 g) pulled pork, chopped

Cajun seasoning

Steamer basket

Preparation

Place 1 cup of chicken broth and the corn in a blender, process until smooth. Set aside.

Combine masa harina, salt and baking powder in a bowl. Stir well with a whisk. Cut in 1/8 cup lard (or bacon fat if lard is unavailable) with a pastry blender until mixture resembles bread crumbs. Add the broth and corn puree and stir well until a soft dough forms. Cover and chill at least 1 hour.

Place corn husks in a large bowl, cover with warm water. Weigh the husks down with a large pot and soak 1 hour.

Melt 1 tablespoon lard in a frying pan at medium-high heat. Add the onion, sauté until brown (approx. 5 minutes). Add the garlic and sauté for a further 2 minutes. Add the remaining cup of broth and bring to a boil. Reduce heat to medium-low and simmer until liquid is reduced to approx. 1/4 cup. Add the pulled pork and toss well. Add Cajun seasoning to taste.

Place approx. 1 rounded tablespoon masa dough on the centre of a husk, pressing into a rectangle, leaving at least 1/2 inch of space on all sides. Place 1 heaped tablespoon of pork mixture on top of the dough. Fold the husk over the filling, covering the meat with dough, fold husk over once more before folding bottom end of husk underneath. Evenly place tamales in a steamer basket positioned in a large pot. Steam 1 hour.

Let them rest 20 minutes and enjoy !

Your personal notes

....

....

....

....

Zwolle NL

Blue fingers from Zwolle

Population : 120.355

Province : Overijssel

Website : www.zwolle.nl

The national anthem from Zwolle states "I am from Zwolle, really from Zwolle, *look at my fingers* I am really from Zwolle"

The myth

It is said that in the Middle Ages the city of Kampen once ordered a number of church bells from its arch rival, Zwolle. The invoice was sent from Zwolle to Kampen, however it was considered far too expensive ! As revenge the Kampen inhabitants paid in 5 cent pieces (pennies). It took days to count the copper and caused blue fingers from the coins in the process!

The possible truth

The folk from Zwolle gained their nickname due to their betrayal of their leader, the bishop of Utrecht. Initially they swore their loyalty to him by raising their forefinger and middle finger into the air.

However, at a later date they changed their allegiance to the enemy, the Duke of Gelre and ever since the people from Zwolle are referred to as *blue fingers*. In the Middle Ages this was a cause for shame, however nowadays the people from Zwolle are proud of their nickname. There are many references to blue fingers in Zwolle, for example blue finger cookies, the blue finger run, a blue finger café, the soccer team players of PEC Zwolle are also called blue fingers and so on ....

Fun USA (music) Fact:

Blue Finger is the title of a CD by Black Francis released in 2007. He was inspired by the Dutch artist Herman Brood, who was born in Zwolle.

Appeltaart

Apple pie

Serves 8—10 p.

Preparation 30 minutes

Baking time 60 minutes

Shopping list

Pastry

2 cups (300 g) all purpose flour

7 oz. (200 g) soft butter

pinch of salt

1/2 cup (125 g) caster sugar

2 small eggs

Filling

6 large apples (slightly sour)

4 tablespoons brown caster sugar

1 teaspoon vanilla sugar

2 teaspoons ground cinnamon

2 tablespoons sultanas (soaked 1 hour)

2 tablespoons currants (soaked 1 hour)

2 rusks

1 spring form cake tin (diameter 24 cm)

Preparation

Sieve de flower and mix in a bowl together with the butter, sugar and one egg, Add a pinch of salt. Knead to a consistent, smooth dough. Put it in the fridge for 30 minutes.

Grease the spring form cake tin. Roll out 3/4 of the dough to cover the bottom and sides of the tin.

Preheat the oven to 338 F/170 C.

Peel, core and slice the apples finely. Mix with the 2 sugars and the cinnamon.

Mix the soaked currants and raisins (well drained and dried) with the apples.

Pulverize the rusks enough to cover the dough base. Place the apple mixture on top of the pulverized rusks.

Roll out the remaining dough and cut into long strips. Place these strips in a lattice form on top of the apple mixture . Press the ends of the strips firmly to the edge of the pie and trim away any excess dough with a knife.

Beat the remaining egg and use it to glaze the lattice strips.

Bake for approx. 60 minutes until pastry is golden brown.

Enjoy !

Photo courtesy of Mr. Hans Hoekstra — www.hanshoekstrafotografie.nl

Herinnering aan Holland

Denkend aan Holland
zie ik breede rivieren
traag door oneindig
laagland gaan,

rijen ondenkbaar
ijle populieren
als hooge pluimen
aan den einder staan;

en in de geweldige
ruimte verzonken
de boerderijen
verspreid door het land,

boomgroepen, dorpen,
geknotte torens,
kerken en olmen
in een grootsch verband.

de lucht hangt er laag
en de zon wordt er
langzaam
in grijze veelkleurige
dampen gesmoord,

en in alle gewesten
wordt de stem van het water
met zijn eeuwige rampen
gevreesd en gehoord.

Hendrik Marsman 1936

(1899—1940)

Uitgeverij Querido

Memory of Holland

Thinking of Holland
I see wide rivers
slugging through
limitless low-lying land,

lines of implausibly
gauzy poplars
like feathered plumes
in far distances stand;

and sunken away
in the formidable vastness
the farmsteads
scattered are found,

tree clumps, villages
pollarded steeples,
churches and elms
in one great design bound.

the sky hangs low there
and in grey vapours of
colour
the sun there,
is slowly blurred,

and in all the regions
the voice of the water
with its eternal disasters
is dreaded and heard.

Hendrik Marsman 1936

Courtesy of Mr. Paul Vincent. His translation won the
David Reid Poetry Translation Prize, Autumn 2006

Holland Amerika Lijn—now Hotel New York in Rotterdam

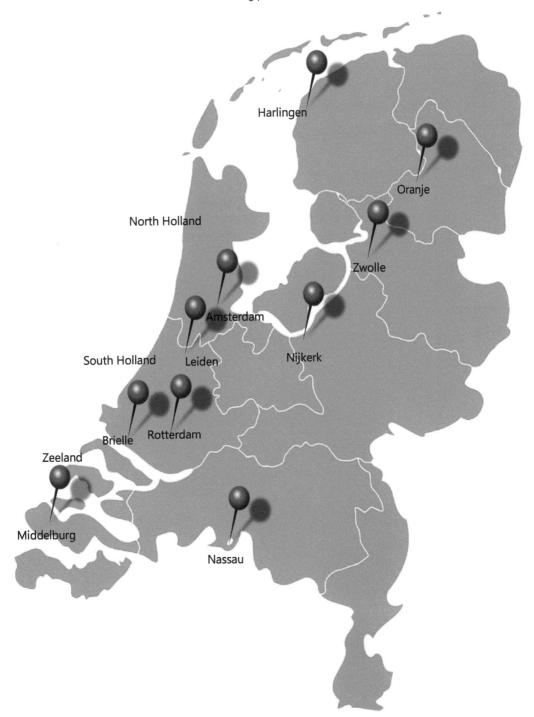

Harlingen

Oranje

North Holland

Zwolle

Amsterdam

Nijkerk

South Holland   Leiden

Brielle   Rotterdam

Zeeland

Middelburg

Nassau

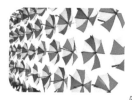

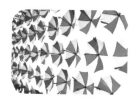

Acknowledgements

There are many people I would like to thank for their help. Without them I could never have been able to create this book.

First of all I would like to thank Conny Thiel for her brilliant ideas at the start of this book and the many, many hours we spent during the first year together both on our own side of the Atlantic ocean exchanging tips, information, ideas and so much more.

Secondly my friend Sally Oosthoek, who—as a native speaker—offered to check my prose and recipes. Whilst correcting my "Dutch" English she also read my texts with a critical eye making sure that the content made sense and occasionally providing tips for improvements. I am really appreciative and most grateful for all the work she has done! (www.so-translations.nl)

Furthermore I would like to mention in order of the cities that appear in the book :

- Amsterdam USA : Two Dutch filmmakers, Rogier van Eck and Rob Rombout, who gave permission to use the drawing of their trip to 15 Amsterdams !

- Brielle USA : Mr. John Belding, Brielle Borough Historian

- Brielle Nl : VVV Brielle

- Harlingen USA : Mrs. Melisa Prine Cortez and Mr. Norman Rozeff

- Holland USA : Mrs. Sinka Babinec, Sally Hallan Laukitis and Holli DeWaard and the Holland Area Convention & Visitors Bureau

- Leyden USA : Mrs. Nicole Glabach, Leyden town clerk

- Middleburg USA : Mr. Vincent Bataoel

- Middelburg Nl : Team Roosevelt Foundation

Acknowledgements

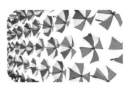

- Nassau Village USA : Mr. Kurt Vincent, President of the Nassau village Historical Society and Mrs. Melody Howarth, Nassau Town historian

- Baarle Nassau : VVV Baarle-Hertog-Nasssau

- Schenectady USA and Nijkerk Nl : Mrs. Edith Terschegget

- Orange City USA : Mr. Mike Hofman— Executive Director, Orange City Chamber of Commerce

- Oranje Nl : Mrs. Esther van het Maalpad, coordinator Tourist info Midden-Drenthe—www.drentsehooglanden.nl

- Rotterdam USA : Mrs. Diane Martin-Supervisor's Office Town of Rotterdam, Mr. Michael Maloney—librarian Schenectady County Historical Society

- Rotterdam NL : Mrs. Hedwig Meesters for the beautiful pictures of the Markthal

- Zeeland USA : Mrs. Dorothy Voss and Zeeland Historical Society, Mrs. Karen Jipping city clerk

- Zeeland Nl : beeldenbank.laatzeelandzien.nl

And of course I must thank my family and friends who were forced to listen to my stories about "the book" every time I discovered something new about a town in the USA and a new *Dutch Connection*. They also had to taste all the recipes and for that I am eternally grateful. Thank you all from the bottom of my heart !

CPSIA information can be obtained
at www.ICGtesting.com
Printed in the USA
LVHW071502221019
634979LV00009B/266/P